MW01227866

PRAISE MY PET!

ADULT COLORING BOOK

WWW.PRAISEMYPET.COM

Copyright

Copyright © 2021 by Praise My Pet

www.praisemypet.com

All rights reserved.

Printed in the United States of America.

Color Lilla and Toby!

Color Roxxy!

3

Color Zoey and Riley!

Color Neda!

Color Gracie!

6

Color Dagmar, Brownie, Handsome, Chance and Pandora!

Color Zorro and Budz McGee!

Color Maxamillian and Bristol!

10

Color Luckypup Pike and Tig!

11

Color Elijah!

Color Jade!

Color Sadie and Izu!

12

Color Willow and Haven!

Color Jack and Hayden!

13

Color Nikko!

16

Color Zoey Luv and April June!

Color Stella!

Color Maximus!

Color Chloe!

18

Color Jackson!

Color Miles and Odie!

20

Color Angel, Regan and Raider!

Color Diesel and Bella!

21

Color Lexie!

Color Cupcake and Harry!

Color Bear and Hercules!

Color Tiger!

Color Smokey!

Color Hunter and Bentley!

Color Oreo and Lily Star!

Color Peanut and Minnie!

Color Pebbles and Sweetpea!

Color Mia, Sparky and Twinkie!

Color Paloma!

Color Mitzi Sue!

Color Tahoe!

33

34

Color Demi and Callie!

Color Gus-Gus!

Color Millie D!

Color Miss Molly and Maxie!

Color Lulu Love, Gizmo and Herbie!

Color Odie!

40

Color Lil Bear and Peanut!

Color Casey, Mimi and Mojo!

Color Ray and Crook!

42

Color Hollywood and Vinne!

Color JoJo!

43

Color Ash and Midnight!

44

Color Uno, Emma, B.B. and Dizzie!

Color Otis Secord Courtney!

Color Cassius!

Color Jax, Joey and Willow!

Color Tito!

46

Color Toren and Keely!

Color Kitty!

47

Color Cooper and Lord Stanley!

Color Walter!

Color Garfield!

51

Color Gizzy!

Color Chewy!

Color Bebee!

52

Color JoJo!

Color Chai, Kula, Hana and Brin!

Color Molly and Onyx!

Color Myla!

54

Color Wally and Jasper!

Color Sunny Boy and Itty!

57

Color Trooper and Snoopy!

Color Brady and Rio!

Color Diamond!

Color Ginger!

Color Tucker!

59

Color Snickers, Cupcake and Peanut!

Color Cookie!

Color Annie and Louie!

Color Unchi and Kitsune!

Color Rachel Belle and Mollie Belle!

64

Color Maggie and Bernie!

Color Finn!

Color Hank and Kiki!

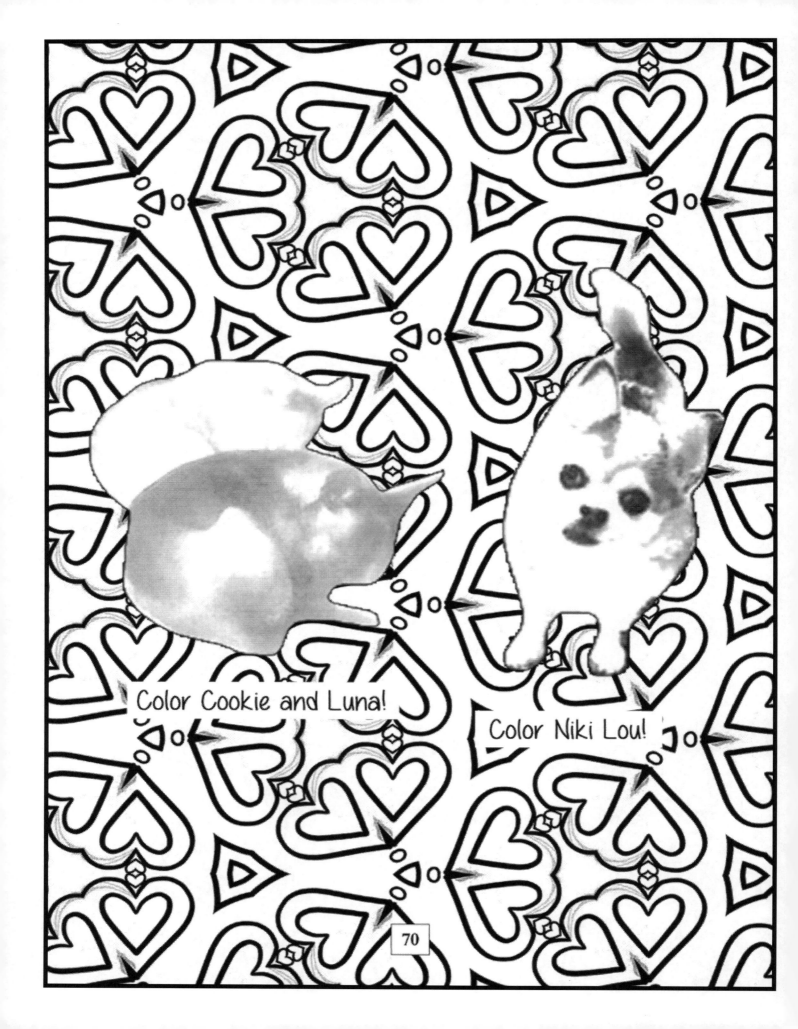

Color Cookie and Luna!

Color Niki Lou!

70

Color Nubbins and Diamond!

Color Charlie and Pebbles!

71

Color Bella, Hazel, Gizmo and Meme!

Color Lucky and Zhasha!

72

Color Linda and Netto!

Color Little Ricky!

Color Muneca and Neo!

Color Poppy!

76

Color Kallie Joe!

78

Color Nikita and Chloe!

Color Lucy Bugg!

Color Zuess!

Color Jessie, Gidget, Buster and Chico!

84

Color Jill Cross Boots!

Color Prancer!

85

86

Color Bogie and Baby!

Color Serenity!

Color Mercedes Miracle!

88

Color Bandit!

Color Lincoln!

89

Color Little Booger!

91

Color Bandit!

Color Pepe and Bella!

Color Marble and Gilbert!

94

Color Daisy!

Color Scooter!

95

Color Zoe and Nala!

96

Color Mr Ree, Ta-Ta and Kudos!

98

Color Sophie!

99

Color Pixie!

100

Color Toodles and Mickey!

Color China Girl and Cookie Jo!

102

We hope you enjoyed our coloring book! If you'd like to see YOUR pet in one of our upcoming coloring books, visit www.praisemypet.com/pages/send-us-your-pet-photos

Happy coloring!

Made in the USA
Columbia, SC
19 February 2021

33229595R00057